**W9-AJP-918**

DATE DUE

AG 12'90			
JUL 14 '94			
JY 13 '01			
MR 2 0 0			
AP 05 04			
MR 08'06			
AG 2 5 14			

DEMCO

MAINE

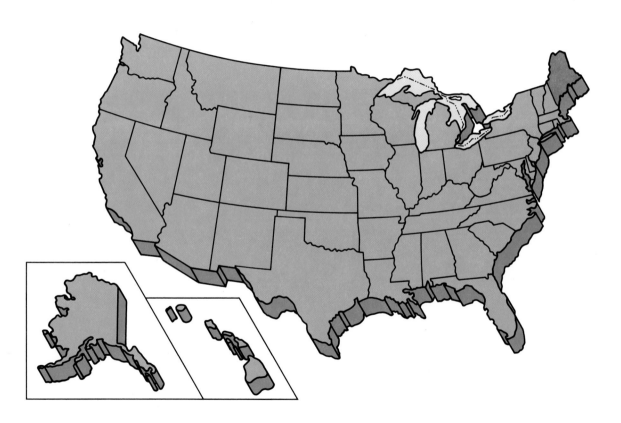

MAINE

LeeAnne Engfer

Lerner Publications Company

LIBRARY OF CONGRESS
CATALOGING-IN-PUBLICATION DATA
Engfer, LeeAnne.
    Maine / LeeAnne Engfer.
        p. cm. — (Hello USA)
    Includes index.
    Summary: Introduces the geography, history, industries, people, and other highlights of Maine.
        ISBN 0-8225-2701-4 (lib. bdg.)
    1. Maine—Juvenile literature.
[1. Maine.] I. Title. II. Series.
F19.3.E54 1991
974.1—dc20   90-38215
                                        CIP
                                         AC

Cover photograph by Benjamin Goldstein / Root Resources.

The glossary on page 69 gives definitions of words shown in **bold type** in the text.

Manufactured in the United States of America

1 2 3 4 5 6 7 8 9 10 99 98 97 96 95 94 93 92 91

 This book is printed on recycled paper.

CONTENTS

Did You Know . . . ?

☐ Northern Maine is a good place to spot a moose. Maine has more moose than any other state besides Alaska. You're most likely to see a moose at dawn or dusk. They hide among the trees, and they stand in shallow lakes and streams eating water plants.

6

❑ George Bush, the 41st president of the United States, makes his summer home in the seaside town of Kennebunkport, Maine.

❑ The L. L. Bean outdoor goods store in Freeport, Maine, is the state's second biggest tourist attraction. Every year about 2.5 million people visit the store, which features an indoor trout pond.

❑ Most of the lobsters we eat come from Maine. The world's largest lobster boiler is in Rockland, Maine. The boiler is 24 feet long (7.3 meters) and can steam 5,000 pounds (2,250 kilograms) of lobster in an hour.

A Trip Around the State

Millions of people visit Maine each year. They are drawn to the state's vast green forests, sparkling lakes, long rivers, rounded mountains, and rocky shores. Sometimes people talk about the "mystique" of Maine—that is, all the things that make the state special, such as the lighthouses, the fog, and the beaches.

Maine, the largest state in the New England region, forms the northeastern tip of the United States. A slim finger of land called West Quoddy Head is the easternmost point in the nation. When you're in Maine, you can see the sun rise before anyone else in the country can.

9

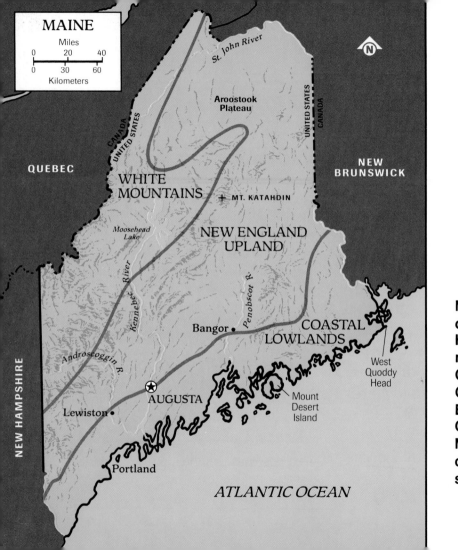

MAINE

Miles
0   20   40
0   30   60
Kilometers

St. John River

N

Aroostook
Plateau

QUEBEC

CANADA
UNITED STATES

UNITED STATES
CANADA

WHITE
MOUNTAINS

NEW
BRUNSWICK

+ MT. KATAHDIN

Moosehead
Lake

NEW ENGLAND
UPLAND

Kennebec River

Penobscot R.

Bangor •

COASTAL
LOWLANDS

West
Quoddy
Head

Androscoggin R.

NEW HAMPSHIRE

☆ AUGUSTA

Mount
Desert
Island

Lewiston •

Portland

ATLANTIC OCEAN

Maine borders only one other state — New Hampshire. Maine's other neighbors are the Canadian provinces of Quebec and New Brunswick. The Atlantic Ocean washes against Maine's long diagonal coast, which runs from southwest to northeast.

During the last **Ice Age,** which began about 80,000 years ago, sheets of ice up to a mile thick covered much of North America. By about 12,000 years ago, these **glaciers** had melted. The slow-moving ice ground down the Coastal Lowlands in southern Maine. The state's two other regions—the New England Upland and the White Mountains—are still hilly.

Melting ice from the glaciers created many lakes throughout the state and caused the sea level to rise. The rising ocean drowned hundreds of mountains and hills. Their peaks now form Maine's islands—there are about 2,000 of them. The largest is Mount Desert Island.

This peaceful pond lies on Mount Desert Island.

It's fun to play on the sandy beaches of southern Maine.

The Coastal Lowlands hug the shoreline along the Atlantic Ocean. The lowlands extend from 10 to 40 miles (16 to 64 kilometers) inland. Maine's coast twists and turns into many bays. Miles of sandy beaches stretch along the southern shores. Farther north, huge rocks jut into the sea.

Mainers call the northeastern part of the coast "Down East," and many people refer to the state itself as Down East. Sailors first used the term in the 1800s when their ships were carried east from Boston toward Maine and Canada.

The fertile soil of the Aroostook Plateau is good for growing crops.

Cutting a band through the middle of the state, the New England Upland region rises from sea level in the east to nearly 2,000 feet (610 m) in the southwest. In the northeastern part of this region lies the Aroostook Plateau—a flat highland with deep, fertile soil.

13

Mount Katahdin is the highest point in Maine.

The White Mountains stretch across northwestern Maine. Mount Katahdin, the highest point in the state, reaches nearly a mile (5,268 feet / 1.6 km) into the sky.

Waterways abound in Maine. There are more than 5,000 lakes and ponds. Moosehead Lake is the largest. At least 5,000 rivers and streams run through the state. The longest rivers include the St. John, Penobscot, Kennebec, and Androscoggin.

The names of many geographical features in Maine come from Indian words. The name *Androscoggin,* for example, means "place where fish are cured." *Katahdin* means "principal mountain."

Woodlands cover almost 90 percent of Maine. Hunters, campers, and hikers have been known to get lost in the far-reaching woods. In northern and eastern Maine, spruce, fir, and white pine trees are common. In the south and central regions, birch, beech, maple, and oak trees grow.

Rich green forests *(left)* and bright flowers such as the purple lupine *(above)* add to Maine's natural colors.

15

Bears, moose, beavers, and white-tailed deer live in Maine. The streams are filled with trout and salmon, and many other kinds of fish and sea creatures swim in the coastal waters. The bald eagle soars above Maine's rivers and woodlands.

16

Winters are very cold in northern Maine, with heavy snowfall and temperatures that plunge below zero. Along the coast, the climate is warmer in the winter and cooler in the summer than it is in the interior. Fog often rolls in from the ocean.

The state gets plenty of rain each year. Storms called **northeasters** whip in from the ocean, creating huge waves.

Maine's Story

Humans have lived on the North American continent since the time when ice covered present-day Maine. These people and their descendants are called Indians, or Native Americans. After the glaciers melted, bands of people entered the area that is now Maine. The major group in Maine was the Abnaki. *Abnaki* means "people of the dawnland."

The Abnaki lived off the natural bounty of the land. In the spring they fished for salmon, bass, and sturgeon in streams and rivers. In the summer they gathered nuts, such as acorns, and picked many kinds of berries. They caught shellfish in the ocean. In the fall they hunted deer, moose, beavers, and bears.

Hunting and Gathering

What did the Indians eat? The answer is simple: everything they could. They gathered a wide variety of plants and nuts and hunted many kinds of animals. At one archaeological site in the northeastern United States, remains of all these foods were found:

beaver	deer	wolf fish	bald eagle
dog	harbor seal	bay scallop	great auk
red fox	snapping turtle	mussel	loon
mink	stingray	long clam	great blue heron
	sturgeon	moon snail	mallard
	sea bass	thick-lipped dill	red-tailed hawk

great auk

Using birchbark, the Abnaki built canoes, which they used for traveling and fishing in lakes and rivers. They made snowshoes to make walking and hunting easier in the winter snow.

Source: *The Smithsonian Book of North American Indians: Before the Coming of the Europeans* by Philip Kopper.

The Abnaki designed wigwams similar to this one, which was built in the early 1900s.

The Abnaki lived in cone-shaped **wigwams** made of animal hides or birch bark. Tribes moved from place to place to find the best food and game. Older Abnaki family members passed down stories and legends to young people, who were taught to respect the land and animals. The Abnaki's way of life lasted for hundreds of years, until white people came to the area.

Columbus's voyage to the Caribbean islands in 1492 inspired many other Europeans to set sail for the "New World." Some explorers made it as far north as Maine.

"New World." One explorer who reached the northeast was John Cabot, who worked for the king of England. England then claimed ownership of the land that Cabot discovered.

Throughout the 1500s, English, Spanish, Italian, and French explorers ventured along the coast of Maine and into the interior. They reported on the natural riches they found—trees, fish, animals, and water.

Around A.D. 1000, Vikings from Scandinavia sailed to the northeastern coast of North America. After Christopher Columbus's voyage to the Americas in 1492, many Europeans set off for this

23

Samuel de Champlain led a French expedition to the northeast coast of America in the early 1600s.

In 1604 two Frenchmen established a **colony** of about 70 people on an island near the border of what is now Maine. After a freezing winter with few supplies, the French settlers returned to France.

British captain George Waymouth was the next European to explore Maine's coast. In 1605 he kidnapped five Abnaki Indians and took them back to Britain with him. Two men who worked for King James I—Sir Ferdinando Gorges and Sir John Popham—questioned the Indians about their home. Using a few English words and lots of gestures, the Abnaki described their beautiful lands.

The earliest British colonists in Maine settled on Popham Beach. Later, in the 1800s, a fort was built on the site of the original settlement.

Convinced that this faraway territory could prove valuable, Gorges and Popham decided to sponsor a settlement there. In 1607 Popham's nephew, George Popham, brought a group of settlers to the mouth of the Kennebec River to build the colony that his uncle wanted. The settlement lasted only a year, however. The settlers lost their leaders when George Popham and John Popham died in 1607.

A few years later, the French returned to the northeast. They settled on Mount Desert Island in 1613, but a British captain drove them off the island. He declared that the island belonged to Britain.

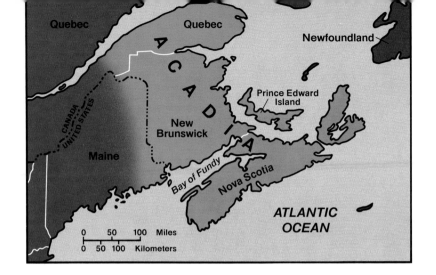

The French colony of Acadia extended from present-day Quebec to eastern Maine and Nova Scotia.

During the next decades, both the French and the British staked out sections of North America for their colonies. The French claimed part of what is now eastern Maine. This land, along with territory in eastern Canada, made up the French colony of Acadia.

In 1622 Britain's king, James I, gave Ferdinando Gorges and John Mason land in Maine. The British built several small settlements in Maine during the 1620s and 1630s. The white settlers carried diseases that were new to the Indians. Smallpox wiped out many Abnaki. In some places, three out of every four died.

The Abnaki tried to keep the British from taking over the land the Indians had lived on for generations. The Indians and British fought often, and many people were killed in bloody battles. The Indians got along better with the French, who traded European goods to the Abnaki for furs.

After Ferdinando Gorges died in 1647, the British-owned Massachusetts Bay Colony claimed Maine as part of its territory. In 1691 Maine became part of Massachusetts.

The British fought the French for control of land in New England on and off from 1689 to 1763. The Abnaki usually sided with the French in these battles. The last conflict, called the French and Indian War, began in 1754. France lost, and the **treaty,** signed in 1763, gave Britain control of most of North America. Many Abnaki fled to Canada. Only a small number of Indians remained in Maine.

Indians fought British soldiers in 1755.

27

Trees were valuable for the settlers of Maine.

Between 1690 and 1760, the white population of Maine increased tenfold. The new settlers, like the Indians before them, made use of the natural resources in the area. The land offered plenty of wood to use for timber and shipbuilding. The colonists built elegant wooden sailing ships and sold them to other colonies. The settlers also fished in the coastal waters.

In 1775 Maine became involved in the American War of Independence. In June, Maine patriots captured a British ship, and the first naval battle of the Revolution was fought at Machias, Maine. Later that year, British troops bombarded the city of Falmouth (now Portland), Maine, with heated cannonballs. Three-fourths of the town burned.

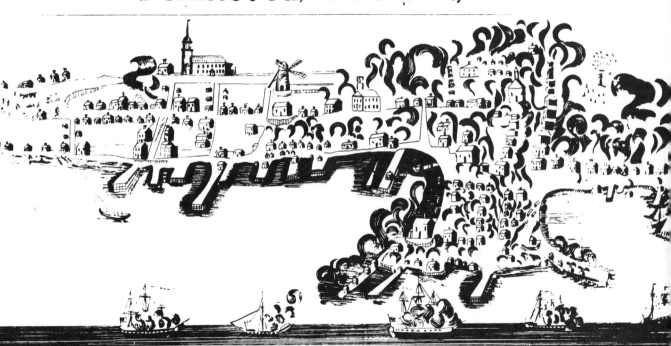

THE TOWN of FALMOUTH, *Burnt by Captain* MOET, Octr 18 1775

A 1791 drawing shows the burning of Falmouth during the Revolutionary War.

Maine's state flag shows
a pine tree, a moose,
a farmer, and a seaman.

After the war ended in 1783, Maine's population continued to grow by leaps and bounds. The Massachusetts government sold land in Maine to settlers for less than a dollar an acre. Many people from Massachusetts and New Hampshire moved to Maine. Between 1783 and 1791, the population of Maine increased by 40,000.

In 1820 Maine separated from Massachusetts and became the 23rd state of the United States. The new state seemed to have a promising future. Its vast wilderness marked a frontier full of possibility.

A sketch shows an early settlement in Maine.

Mainers continued to rely on shipbuilding and lumber to make a living. Each year from December through May, lumberjacks lived in Maine's forests. They cut pine logs, hauled them by sled, and piled them next to the Kennebec and Penobscot rivers.

In March or April, during "ice out," the ice on the river broke up. Lumberjacks threw the logs into the river, and the river current carried them downstream to sawmills near the seaports. Maine sold a lot of lumber to other states.

Loggers haul timber on a horse-drawn sleigh. Lumbering has been a source of jobs in Maine for more than three centuries.

Textile and leather factories began operating in Maine in the 1800s. Shown here is a shoe factory in Yarmouth in 1910.

In the mid-1800s, textile (cloth) and leather factories opened throughout New England, including Maine. Lumbering and fishing, however, remained the state's best money-makers.

By the mid-1800s, most of Maine's Abnaki Indians had been forced to live on reservations. Many Abnaki still live on this land.

A new industry sprang up in the late 1800s—paper. Between 1868 and 1900, paper mills opened in several towns in Maine, such as Mechanic Falls, Westbrook, and Yarmouth. Many paper mills used rivers for **hydropower**—a cheap form of electricity—to run their machines.

Thousands of French Canadians crossed the border to find jobs in Maine's textile mills. Soon a large community of French Americans lived in Maine. **Immigrants** from other countries, such as Ireland, came to the state, too.

As white people settled on more territory, the original inhabitants of Maine—the Indians—lost almost all of their land. By the 1850s, most Indians lived on just a couple of **reservations,** areas of land set aside for them.

Throughout the mid- to late 1800s, many farmers left Maine and moved west, where the land was better for farming. This trend continued into the 1900s.

After the invention of the steamship, sailboats were used more for pleasure than for transportation.

Some industries also declined during this period. After the invention of the steamboat, demand for sailing ships fell. This hurt Maine's shipbuilding industry. The state also lost many textile mills when they were moved to southern states, where cloth could be produced more cheaply. But Maine continued to make more and more paper products.

By 1900 people from other states were beginning to discover some of the mystique of Maine—its unspoiled beauty and lack of crowded cities. Maine Central Railroad opened a ticket office in New York City and ran newspaper advertisements encouraging New Yorkers to visit Maine.

In the early 1900s, many people discovered that Maine was an ideal place for a vacation.

37

Although tourists brought a lot of money into the state, many Mainers faced hard times in the 1900s. Maine never had much heavy industry. This helped keep the state clean and the population low, but it also meant that for many Mainers, finding a job was tough. The traditional activities—lumbering, fishing, and farming—did not provide enough jobs for everyone who wanted a job.

Digging for clams *(facing page)* and other fishing activities along Maine's coast became less common in the 1900s. Lumbering *(right)* is still an important industry in Maine, but most people now work in service jobs.

5,000 B.C.   **A.D. 1000**   **1607**   **1691**   **1754**

- **5,000 B.C.** — First humans arrive in what is now Maine
- **A.D. 1000** — Vikings reach the northeast coast of North America
- **1607** — The Popham colony, the first settlement in Maine, is established
- **1691** — Maine becomes part of the Massachusetts Bay Colony
- **1754** — Mainers begin fighting in the French and Indian War (1754–1763)

In the 1980s, however, the state's economy improved. Many new service jobs were created in businesses such as retail stores, restaurants, and government. Land along the coast increased in value. New homes, offices, and factories were built. By the end of the decade, there were many jobs in the state's largest city, Portland. After a century of hardship, Mainers felt as if they could make a living in the state.

1820

1900

1980

American Revolutionary War (1775–1783) begins

Maine becomes the 23rd state to join the Union

Tourism takes hold as a big business in Maine

Maine Indian Claims Act awards land and money to Maine's Native Americans

In 1980 President Jimmy Carter signed the Maine Indian Claims Settlement Act. The new law gave Maine's native people money both to buy land and to save for future generations.

41

Living and Working in Maine

Compared to most other states, the number of people who live in Maine is small—just over one million. In the northern part of the state in particular, towns are few and far between. In Maine you can get away from busy cities and crowds of people. This is part of Maine's mystique.

Portland *(left)* **is Maine's largest city.** *Facing page:* **Mainers come from a variety of backgrounds.**

Almost half of the people in Maine live in urban areas. Most people live along the coast. The state's largest city is Portland, with 62,000 people. Other large communities include Lewiston, Bangor, and Augusta, the capital.

Almost all Mainers were born in the United States. Their ancestors came mostly from Britain, France, and Canada. In some towns near the Canadian border, many residents still speak French.

About 4,000 Native Americans live in Maine. The two major groups, the Penobscot and the Passamaquoddy, are descendants of the original Abnaki.

A dietary aide prepares a meal at Maine Medical Center in Portland. Jobs in hospitals are one kind of service.

Most people in Maine work in jobs that provide a service. Service businesses include stores, restaurants, motels, schools, and hospitals. Government is another important service. Altogether, these businesses account for about 70 percent of the money that people in the state make each year.

Another big part of Maine's economy is manufacturing—the making of goods. Paper products earn more money than any other good manufactured in the state. Paper companies make newsprint for newspapers and glossy paper for magazines, as well as facial tissues and paper towels.

Farmers in Aroostook County harvest potatoes, Maine's most valuable crop.

Many Mainers work in the forest-products industry. They cut down trees, haul logs, and make wood products. Besides lumber and paper, some wood items made in Maine include matches, toys, and furniture. Maine makes more toothpicks than any other state.

Although farming is not a large part of Maine's economy, some farm products are important. Dairy farms dot the countryside. Potatoes—grown in the rich soil of the Aroostook Plateau—are the state's most valuable farm crop. Maine's potato output is third in the nation, after Idaho and Washington. More blueberries are grown in Maine than in any other state in the country.

47

A lobsterman checks to see if his catch is a female. Female lobsters are thrown back into the ocean because they are needed to lay eggs and produce more lobsters.

Maine is famous for its lobsters. Lobster boats and lobster shacks are a common sight along the coast. Lobstermen haul in about 22 million pounds (10 million kg) of lobster each year. Clams, cod, flounder, and other fish and shellfish add to Maine's annual seafood harvest.

Factories in Maine freeze or can foods to be sold throughout the country. The state's farmers send apples, potatoes, and blueberries to factories where they are made into juice, french fries, and other foods. Workers at plants package chicken and can sardines and other seafood.

A Few Facts about Lobsters

The lobster is a *crustacean.* Crustaceans are animals that have hard shells and no backbones. The lobster's hard shell covers its body like a suit of armor. Lobsters' shells are dark green or blue, and they turn red when they're cooked. Lobsters have two large claws that extend out in front, four pairs of legs for walking, and a tail that spreads out like a fan.

Lobsters live on the bottom of the ocean near shore. They hide in holes or under rocks. The lobster fisherman traps lobsters in cages called *pots,* which are lowered to the ocean floor. Fish are placed in the pots as bait. The lobster can walk into the trap but can't find its way out. The fisherman hauls the traps up from the bottom of the sea with a strong cord that connects the trap to a buoy that floats on the surface of the water.

The pots are left in the water for a day or two. Then the lobster fisherman hauls the traps, removes his catch, adds new bait, and returns the pots to the bottom. People who make their living from fishing for lobster use anywhere from 400 to 1,000 traps.

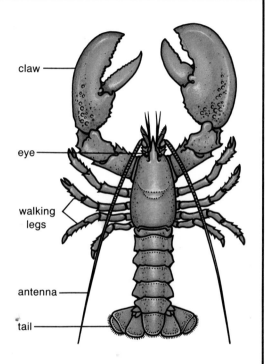

An average Maine lobster weighs about 1.5 pounds (0.7 kg), but some deepwater lobsters weigh as much as 20 pounds (9 kg).

Tourism provides many jobs for Mainers. Each year, millions of people travel to Maine, where they discover what makes the state special. Acadia National Park on Mount Desert Island draws many visitors.

Tourists also flock to the coast, with its white lighthouses and salty air, or they head north to the forests, lakes, and mountains. Many people visit the woods in autumn, when the leaves burst into a brilliant display of yellow, red, and orange.

Maine offers a range of fun things to do and see. Some activities include *(left to right)* folk dancing at the New Sweden Historical Museum, "spud wrestling" in mashed potatoes at the Potato Festival in Fort Fairfield, sailing, cross-country skiing, and hiking and camping.

In many towns in Maine, you can visit a historical building or a museum. Mainers host a variety of special events, such as the Houlton Potato Feast and the Maine Seafoods Festival. Near Moosehead Lake, 100 teams compete in a dog-sledding race each winter.

52

For nature lovers, Maine offers plenty to do. You can hike, camp, fish, sail, swim, bicycle, or go rock climbing in the summer. In the winter, Mainers and tourists enjoy downhill and cross-country skiing, ice skating, snowmobiling, and ice fishing.

53

Protecting the Environment

For Mainers, the state's beautiful seashores, forests, lakes, and rivers provide a sense of identity and pride as well as a source of money and jobs. For visitors, Maine is a place to enjoy the wilderness and the clean waterways. But, like other states, Maine faces threats to its environment.

One environmental issue for Maine is to keep its shores and coastal waters clean. The coast is home to many kinds of birds, plants, animals, and fish. Many people earn money by fishing in the ocean. Tourists and residents alike appreciate the scenery along the coast.

Maine's coast is home to many plants and animals, including these harbor seals.

Many new homes and businesses are being constructed along Maine's southern coast.

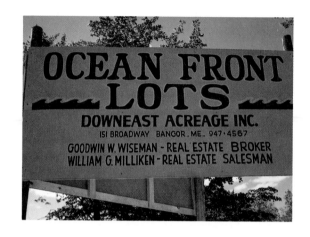

More and more people are moving to Maine's southern coast. Even though the coast is only a small part of all the land in Maine, almost two-thirds of the state's people live and work there. The growth in population has led to a lot of development, or building. Some of this development interferes with the environment.

For example, the risk of water pollution increases. Water pollution comes from several sources. Sometimes the source is obvious, such as tankers that spill oil or factories that dump waste into the sea.

Other times, however, the source of pollution is not as clear. Some everyday activities can also pollute the ocean. Pollutants such as lawn and garden fertilizers, animal wastes, and salts used on icy roads wash into drains and eventually into the ocean.

People and buildings crowd Maine's oceanfront beaches.

Litter and household wastes can also pollute water. Fish get tangled in plastic bags and containers. Birds eat small pieces of plastic. Some scientists say that the plastic yokes that hold six-packs of soda pop will last for 400 years!

When many houses are built along a stretch of Maine's coast, some animals lose their natural habitat. Some species, such as the bird called the puffin, are in danger of extinction—they may not exist in the future.

Maine is taking steps to protect its shores and to keep its water from becoming more polluted.

Each year during Coastweek, thousands of volunteers pick up trash along the coast. In 1989 these citizens collected more than 100,000 items—including 498 six-pack yokes and 7,971 plastic bags.

Various organizations help people who own land along Maine's coast to keep the water clean. The state government has passed laws against dumping waste into the ocean. Other laws determine how coastal land can be used. For example, new factories or homes can be built in some areas, but the state has set aside other land especially for wildlife.

The puffin *(left)* could lose its home if the coast gets overcrowded. Unique plants, such as beach peas *(above)*, also grow along the coast.

59

Volunteers help pick up litter along Maine's coast.

All of Maine's citizens can help out by picking up litter along the coast, by recycling trash, and by learning how to cut down on activities that cause pollution.

Mainers know that their natural resources are valuable. Everyone can work together to protect the environment and to keep Maine beautiful.

Maine's Famous People

Winslow Homer (1836–1910) was a painter celebrated for his powerful seascapes. He made his home in Prout's Neck, Maine.

John Marin (1870–1953) was one of the first American artists to paint in a modern style. His watercolor and oil paintings capture the windblown seascapes and landscapes of Maine. He died in Addison, Maine.

Andrew Wyeth (born 1917) is an artist who spends summers in Cushing, Maine. Wyeth's paintings often depict people and places in rural Maine.

WINSLOW ► HOMER

JOAN BENOIT ▼
SAMUELSON

◄ LOUIS SOCKALEXIS

ATHLETES

Joan Benoit Samuelson (born 1957) grew up in Cape Elizabeth, Maine. A runner, Benoit won the Boston Marathon in 1979 and 1982 and a gold medal for the marathon in the 1984 Summer Oympics. She also won the America's Marathon in 1985.

Louis Sockalexis (1871–1913), born in Old Town, Maine, played professional baseball for the Cleveland Spiders from 1897 to 1899. The team was later renamed the Cleveland Indians in honor of Sockalexis, a Penobscot Indian.

BUSINESS LEADERS

Leon Leonwood (L. L.) Bean (1873–1967), born near Bethel, Maine, founded the nationally known L.L. Bean store, which sells outdoor clothing and gear. The store is in Freeport, Maine.

Milton Bradley (1836–1911), born in Vienna, Maine, was a pioneer in the game business. In 1864 he founded the Milton Bradley Company, which makes popular board games such as Life, Chutes and Ladders, and Candyland.

L. L. BEAN ▶

MILTON BRADLEY ▲

EXPLORERS

Samuel de Champlain (1567–1635), a French explorer, built a colony at the mouth of the St. Croix River and named Mount Desert Island. In 1607 Champlain led a group of settlers to Quebec and founded a colony there.

Giovanni da Verrazano (1485?–1528), an Italian explorer, was one of the first Europeans to explore the coast of Maine.

MISCELLANEOUS

Samantha Smith (1972–1985) was born in Houlton, Maine. When she was 10 years old, she wrote a letter to Soviet leader Yuri Andropov and visited the U.S.S.R. as his guest. She later died in a plane crash.

Percy LeBaron Spencer (1894–1970), born in Howland, Maine, invented the microwave oven in 1946.

SAMANTHA SMITH ▲

George Herbert Walker Bush (born 1924), a summer resident of Kennebunkport, Maine, became the 41st president of the United States in 1989. Bush also served as a U.S. representative, as ambassador to the United Nations (UN), as director of the Central Intelligence Agency (CIA), and as vice-president under Ronald Reagan.

◀ GEORGE BUSH

MARGARET CHASE SMITH
▼

EDMUND MUSKIE ▼

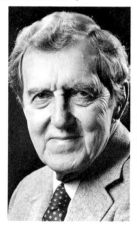

Hannibal Hamlin (1809–1891) was born in Paris Hill, Maine. Hamlin was vice-president of the United States from 1861 to 1865, during Abraham Lincoln's first term. Hamlin strongly opposed slavery.

Edmund Muskie (born 1914) came from Rumford, Maine. Muskie ran for vice-president of the United States in 1968 (along with Hubert Humphrey as presidential candidate), but they lost the race. Muskie was the first Democrat from Maine to serve in the U.S. Congress.

Margaret Chase Smith (born 1897) grew up in Skowhegan, Maine. She was the first woman elected to both houses of the U.S. Congress. Smith was a member of the House of Representatives before she served in the Senate from 1949 to 1973.

Stephen King (born 1947), who is from Bangor, Maine, is a novelist. King writes many popular horror novels, including *Carrie*, *The Shining*, *Salem's Lot*, and *Cujo*.

STEPHEN KING ▶

◀ HENRY WADSWORTH LONGFELLOW

Henry Wadsworth Longfellow (1807–1882), born in Portland, Maine, was a famous poet in the United States during the 1800s. His works include *Evangeline*, *The Song of Hiawatha*, and *The Courtship of Miles Standish*.

Edna St. Vincent Millay (1892–1950) was born in Rockland, Maine. Millay was the first American woman to win the Pulitzer prize for poetry.

Edwin Arlington Robinson (1869–1935), born in Head Tide, Maine, was a poet. Among his books of poetry are *The Man Who Died Twice* and *Tristram*.

◀ E. B. WHITE

E. B. White (1899–1985), an author and humorist, wrote *Charlotte's Web*, *Stuart Little*, and *Trumpet of the Swan*. White spent much of his life on his farm in Allen Cove, Maine.

65

Facts-at-a-Glance

Nickname: Pine Tree State
Song: "State of Maine Song"
Motto: *Dirigo* (I Direct)
Flower: white pine cone and tassel
Tree: white pine
Bird: chickadee
Fish: landlocked salmon
Cat: Maine coon cat

Population: 1,212,000 (1990 estimate)
Rank in population, nationwide: 38th
Area: 33,265 sq mi (86,156 sq km)
Rank in area, nationwide: 39th
Date and ranking of statehood:
   March 15, 1820, the 23rd state
Capital: Augusta
Major Cities (and populations*):
   Portland (62,670), Lewiston (38,980), Bangor
   (30,160), Auburn (22,870), South Portland
   (21,620), Augusta (20,640)
U.S. Senators: 2
U.S. Representatives: 2
Electoral votes: 4

*1986 estimates

Places to visit: Old Gaol Museum in York, Portland Head Light near Portland, Wedding Cake House in Kennebunk, Acadia National Park, Fort Western in Augusta

Annual events: Windjammer Days at Boothbay Harbor (July), Clam Festival in Yarmouth (July), Blueberry Festival in Union (Aug.), Maine Seafood Festival in Rockland (Aug.), Maine State Fair in Lewiston (Sept.)

Natural resources: fertile soil, forests, granite, limestone, stone, garnet

Agricultural products: potatoes, milk, eggs, hay, poultry, beef cattle, apples, blueberries

Manufactured goods: paper products, leather products, lumber and wood products, food products, electrical machinery and equipment, clothing, textiles, rubber and plastic products, transportation equipment

ENDANGERED SPECIES
Mammals—humpback whale, finback whale, eastern cougar
Birds—bald eagle, peregrine falcon, least tern, grasshopper sparrow, sedge wren, piping plover
Reptiles—leatherback turtle, box turtle
Plants—green spleenwort, bushy aster, wild indigo, dwarf white birch, water stargrass, American stickweed, alpine azalea, Jacob's ladder, chestnut oak, flatleaf willow, small whorled pogonia, furbish lousewort

WHERE MAINERS WORK
Services—50 percent
   (services includes jobs in trade; community, social, & personal services; finance, insurance, & real estate; transportation, communication, & utilties)
Manufacturing—22 percent
Agriculture—5 percent
Government—18 percent
Construction—5 percent

CONST 5%
AGR 5%
GOVT 18%
MFG 22%
SERVICES 50%

PRONUNCIATION GUIDE

Abnaki (ab-NAH-kee)

Acadia (uh-KAY-dee-uh)

Aroostook (uh-ROOS-tuhk)

Androscoggin (an-druh-SKAWG-uhn)

Houlton (HOHLT-uhn)

Katahdin (kuh-TAWD-uhn)

Kennebec (kehn-uh-BEHK)

Kennebunkport
   (kehn-uh-BUHNK-port)

Machias (muh-CHEYE-uhs)

Passamaquoddy
   (PAS-uh-muh-KWAWD-ee)

Penobscot (puh-NAWB-skuht)

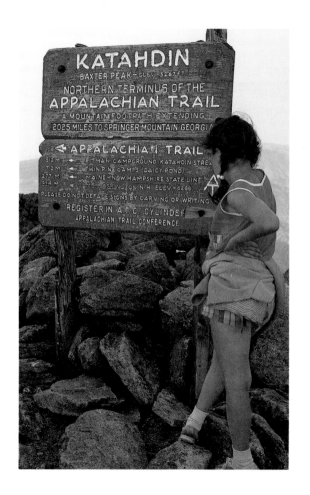

Glossary

colony A territory ruled by a country some distance away.

glacier A large body of ice and snow that moves slowly over land.

hydropower The electricity produced by using waterpower. Also called hydro-electric power.

ice age A period when ice sheets covered large regions of the earth. The term *Ice Age* usually refers to the most recent one, called the Pleistocene, which began almost 2 million years ago and ended about 10,000 years ago.

immigrant A person who moves to a foreign country and settles there.

northeaster A strong storm or wind that blows in from the northeast.

reservation Public land set aside by the government to be used by Native Americans.

treaty An agreement between two or more groups, usually having to do with peace or trade.

wigwam A kind of tent used by some American Indians, shaped in a dome or cone and covered with bark, grass-woven mats, leaves, or other material.

69

Index

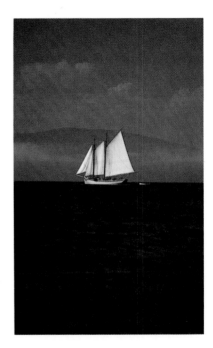